# better together*

*This book is best read together, grownup and kid.

 **akidsco.com**

# a
# kids
# book
# about

# a
# kids
# book
# about
# DIWALI

by Chhavi Arya Bhargava

**A Kids Co.**
**Editor** Emma Wolf
**Designer** Rick DeLucco
**Creative Director** Rick DeLucco
**Studio Manager** Kenya Feldes
**Sales Director** Melanie Wilkins
**Head of Books** Jennifer Goldstein
**CEO and Founder** Jelani Memory

**DK**
**Delhi Technical Team** Bimlesh Tiwary Pushpak Tyagi, Rakesh Kumar
**Senior Production Editor** Jennifer Murray
**Senior Production Controller** Louise Minihane
**Senior Acquisitions Editor** Katy Flint
**Acquisitions Project Editor** Sara Forster
**Managing Art Editor** Vicky Short
**Managing Director, Licensing** Mark Searle

First American edition, 2025
Published in the United States by DK Publishing, 1745 Broadway, 20th Floor,
New York, NY 10019

First published in Great Britain in 2025 by
Dorling Kindersley Limited, 20 Vauxhall Bridge Road, London SW1V 2SA
A Penguin Random House Company

The authorised representative in the EEA is
Dorling Kindersley Verlag GmbH. Arnulfstr. 124, 80636 Munich, Germany

A catalog record for this book is available from the Library of Congress.
A CIP catalogue record for this book is available from the British Library.
ISBN: 978-0-2417-4388-1

DK books are available at special discounts when purchased in bulk for sales
promotions, premiums, fund-raising, or education use. For details, contact:
DK Publishing Special Markets, 1745 Broadway, 20th Floor, New York, NY 10019
SpecialSales@dk.com

Printed and bound in China
**www.dk.com**
**akidsco.com**

For my 2 monkeys,
Rohan and Jaiden
(*ooh-ooh-ah-ah!*).

# Intro
# for grownups

**T**his book is about helping kids and grownups better understand the Diwali holiday, its cultural roots, and traditions. Holidays are a time for celebration, and when kids understand what we are celebrating and why, they feel included in the joy.

Have you ever been curious about how holidays are celebrated around the world? Diwali, the festival of lights, has been celebrated by Hindus, Jains, Sikhs, and Buddhists across South Asia and many other countries over the past 2,500 years. Each person has their own way of celebrating this festival.

This book is here to give a brief introduction to the significance of Diwali and how it's often celebrated. At the heart of Diwali lies the victory of goodness over evil, light over darkness, knowledge over ignorance, and justice over inequality—which is definitely worth celebrating.

**Hi there! My name is Chhavi.**
(You say it like Chuh-vee—
it rhymes with "lovey dovey"!)

And I celebrate Diwali.
दिवाली

Some people say
Diwali (Di-Vah-Lee),
and others say Deepavali
(Dee-pah-va-lee).

"Deep" means light,
and "avali" means row.

# So, Diwali* means a row of lights!

*Diwali is celebrated by Hindus, Sikhs, Jains, and Buddhists, and sometimes they use different names for it! Sikhs call the day Bandi Chor Divas to honor the Sikh struggle for freedom. In Sanskrit, it's known as Deepavali.

# Have you celebrated Diwali before?

It's like Christmas, New Year's, and Independence Day all together!

Every year, my mom would give me

# special sweets

to share with my teachers and friends, but no one understood what they were for or even wished me a happy Diwali.

Do you know any kids who celebrate Diwali?

# MAYBE YOU'RE THAT KID!

I think it's important that everyone can celebrate the holidays which are meaningful to them and their culture.

Being with others who celebrate and understand Diwali makes me feel accepted and like I **belong.**

So, what is Diwali? And what does celebrating it look like?

# Great questions!

But before we get into that, I'll tell you a story...

It's called the Ramayana,* which is about Prince Ram, his wife, Sita, and his loyal brother, Lakshman.

*The stories behind these celebrations depend on the region. The Ramayana is the Hindu story told in most of Northern India. In Southern India, the story honors Lord Krishna's victory over the demon Narakasura. Each story has a similar theme which unites them—the victory of good over evil.

Ram was banished to the forest for 14 years by his stepmother, so that her own son could become king instead.

But Prince Ram did not
go to the forest alone—
Sita and Lakshman
went with him.

A powerful
10-headed king
named Ravana also
lived in the forest.

One day, Ravana kidnapped
Princess Sita and escaped
on his flying chariot back
to the island of Lanka.

But the princess cleverly left a trail of jewelry so she could be found.

Ram and Lakshman followed the jewelry until they met their friend Hanuman, the flying monkey king, who, along with his army, agreed to help find Sita.

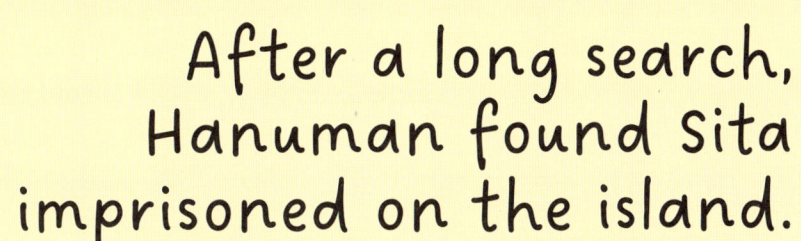

After a long search, Hanuman found Sita imprisoned on the island.

The army of monkeys couldn't reach her, so they built a bridge, and all the animals of the kingdom came to help.

They crossed the bridge and began a legendary battle, finally defeating Ravana with a magical arrow shot from Prince Ram's bow.

Ram and Sita were
reunited and began
their long journey back
to their land, Ayodhya.

It was very dark, so everyone in the city lit oil lamps called *diyas* and placed them in rows to help guide Ram, Sita, and Lakshman home.

The Ramayana teaches us that good will triumph over evil—that light shines through darkness.

# And that's what Diwali is all about!

Diwali is a 5-day celebration.

It takes place in October or November—when the sky is the darkest, on the night of the new moon.

# The 1st day of Diwali is called Dhanteras.

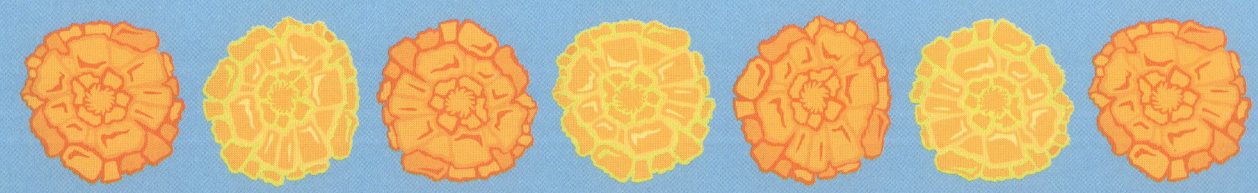

To celebrate, we clean our homes to welcome our guests. Traditionally, families buy something new—like gold or jewelry—to bring good luck and happiness for the whole year. We also make lots of Indian snacks and sweets!

The 2nd day of Diwali is called Choti (small) Diwali.

We decorate our home with rangoli (colored patterns made on the floor with flowers, bright powder, lentils, rice, or sand).

Sometimes we put string lights outside of our house. In many parts of the world, streets are lit with colorful lights.

# The 3rd day is Diwali.

We wear our finest clothes and do a puja (prayer) with family at home or in a temple. We offer foods, sweets, flowers, water, money, and light to God. At the end of the puja, we sing a song called Aarti while holding a diya.

We put a diya in every room, symbolizing that light is more powerful than darkness.

Many Hindus (like me) pray to Goddess Lakshmi for good fortune in the coming year, and Lord Ganesh to help remove any obstacles.*

*Some folks pray to other gods and goddesses for strength and protection.

After this, we receive blessings from our elders, sometimes symbolized with

 **a little mark**

on the forehead, and then we get gifts!

In our family, we reenact the story of the Ramayana, but we make it a bit more modern and funny.

I'm often cast as Surpanakha, who is the mean and jealous sister of the demon king, Ravana, but I don't mind.*

*We told a very short version of the Ramayana earlier. There are a lot more characters, like Surpanakha, in the full story!

The kids love playing Hanuman,
the flying monkey warrior.

OOH-OOH-

# AH-AH!

We play games, have a huge feast (usually vegetarian), dance, party, and light the sky with fireworks*!

*Some people celebrate an eco-friendly version of Diwali without fireworks to reduce pollution.

Many consider the 4th day of Diwali the first day of the new year.

We take this time to be

**grateful for**

**and help others who**

# all we have
## are less fortunate.

The 5th day of Diwali is called Bhai Duj, which means Brother's Day.

It's a day for siblings and cousins to come together, share a meal, and spend time playing games.

Diwali is an important celebration to me, my family, and people all over the world.

# And Diwali is for everyone.

You don't have to celebrate in order to wish someone a **Happy Diwali!**

Try some of the foods and sweets that come with the holiday— they're really yummy!

Ask questions, light a candle,* and share what you've learned.

*Please never light a candle without help from a grownup.

When people feel acknowledged and seen, it means so much to them.

# HAPPY DIWALI!

# Outro
# for grownups

There are lots of fun things you can do to celebrate Diwali. Here are some of our family's favorite activities:

- **DIY diyas:** Decorate and paint your own diyas using clay or dough.
- **Rangoli art:** Create colorful patterns and designs on the floor using chalk, colored sand, rice, lentils, and flower petals.
- **Eat:** Visit a South Asian restaurant or grocery store and try sweets such as ladoo, barfi, peda, gulab jamun, and shakarpara.
- **Color:** Find Diwali-themed coloring pages with beautiful mandalas.
- **Role-play:** Reenact the 5 days of Diwali or the Ramayana.
- **Dance:** Learn a group folk circle dance (raas/garba) with rotating partners.
- **Dress up:** Wear colorful clothes, learn how to tie a sari, or get a henna tattoo.
- **Watch a movie:** I recommend *Kabhi Khushi Khabie Gham*!
- **Attend a celebration:** Find a local festival and join in the fun.
- **Gifts:** Give gifts like baked sweets and diyas to your friends, family, and teachers.
- **Charity:** Donate food or clothes, honoring the importance of giving during Diwali.
- **Learn more:** Download free Diwali resources for home or classroom use at www.bookaboutdiwali.com.

# About The Author

Chhavi Arya Bhargava (she/her) wrote this book to share one of the oldest stories in the world. Diwali is a big part of her identity. When she was a kid, it was a time for family bonding, gift-giving, and eating lots of sweets. It still is!

But no one else outside of her family celebrated or even knew what Diwali was.

When Chhavi got older and became a teacher, she taught kids in school all about respecting every culture and not being afraid to ask questions.

Her hope is that this book showcases some of the wonder and happiness in how families everywhere enjoy Diwali and promotes a feeling of belonging and pride among kids who already celebrate. Chhavi dreams of a future where Diwali can be recognized, appreciated, and understood by kids and grownups everywhere—no matter which holidays they celebrate.

 @chhavidc    @chhavibhargava    bookaboutdiwali.com

# Made to empower.

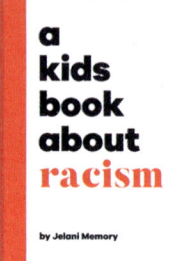

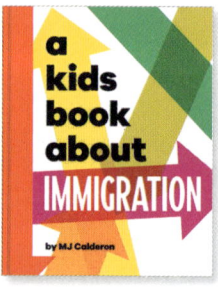

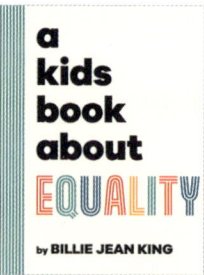

## Discover more at akidsco.com